# *shifting sands*

## THRIVING AT THE EDGE OF CHANGE

*An Employee Handbook*

WILLIAM J. MORIN

SHERRY CADORETTE

**DBM**
**PUBLISHING**

A DIVISION OF DRAKE BEAM MORIN, INC.

Requests for permission to make copies of any part of the
work should be mailed to: Permissions, DBM Publishing,
a Division of Drake Beam Morin, Inc., 100 Park Avenue,
New York, NY 10017 or 1-800-345-5627, FAX 212-972-2120.

Cover photograph by Hugh Sitton/Tony Stone Images
Book design by Katrinka Blickle

Printed and bound in the United States of America
ISBN 1-880030-46-2

# CONTENTS

# INTRODUCTION

YOU'RE PROBABLY reading this booklet because your company has just introduced — or is about to make — a major change. There may be an "r" word involved: restructuring, realignment, re-engineering, reduction-in-force, or right-sizing. Or the change may have been born with a name of its own: "Operation Fresh Start," perhaps, or "Fast Break," or "New Directions 2001."

Whatever it's called, if you're like most people, you find the prospect of change unsettling. Not many of us are really prepared for change when it occurs, and even fewer genuinely welcome it. We tend to approach change with varying degrees of uncertainty, mistrust, and dislike.

But there's no way to avoid change in life, and certainly no way to evade it in business life today. There are ways to deal with the situation, however, methods for tempering its troublesome implications and reinforcing its positive aspects. While we usually can't control change, we can control our reactions to it.

Learning to react to, live with, and ultimately take advantage of change has become a valuable skill, not only at work but in all parts of our lives. After all, if you think about any significant aspect of life today, almost immediately you think about change.

Change is everywhere: at home, school, work, play. The number of families in which both parents work continues to grow as the number of two–parent families continues to decline. Schools are called on to deal with issues that were exclusively family matters a generation ago. The workplace — public or private, profit–driven or not-for-profit — looks and feels like an alien planet to people who retired from it only a few years ago. Today, when people leave work at the end of the day, they have less time for play, but more options to choose from. Everything changes, and the pace of change continues to accelerate. As our cover picture of sand dunes illustrates, our day-to-day environment seems to constantly shift in new and unexpected patterns.

We embrace change and we avoid it, often at the same time. We compete for a promotion at work, and then, having won the position (or even as we strive for it), we're racked with concerns about what might go wrong, with worries about losing the friendship of former colleagues, with thoughts about whether all this is what we really wanted in the first place. We enjoy the challenge of building castles in the sand, knowing that they are vulnerable to changing again with the evening tide.

In the midst of such uncertainty, there is at least one thing with which we should all agree: change isn't going away. To the contrary, change is sure to assume a prominent role in all our lives. It can even offer us a way to view our world differently — with discovery, creativity and hope. Beyond surviving the danger of change there is the potential for thriving with the opportunity of change. Learning and experiementation are often unexpected benefits.

How we deal with change affects both our effectiveness and our general satisfaction in our career and our work environment.  In addition, since what happens at work affects other aspects of life, our response to change at work typically impacts our private life — and the people who are important to us — as well.

This booklet offers a perspective for understanding and reacting to change, and provides suggestions for interpreting and managing the events that surround change. Scattered throughout the pages are metaphors quoted from employees who are living in organizations which are changing. They have been collected from change workshops DBM has conducted over the years.

The employees were asked to describe their feelings and experiences of being inside corporate change. We think they illustrate the paradoxes and conflict change often brings. We hope, too, that they honor the struggle of employees during change and salute their courage in moving forward.

This booklet doesn't propose to offer the final word on change, but, used with other resources that your company may make available, the information introduced here can help you take advantage of a very uncomfortable situation and turn it into your ultimate advantage.

*welcome*

TO

CONSTANT

CHANGE

## THE WAKE-UP CALL

**IT'S 10:00 A.M.** You and your co-workers are assembled in a large meeting room at work, where you've been called to hear "an important announcement." One of your company's top managers — maybe even the president or CEO — is talking. You hear the words ("This is a great opportunity that will make our future much brighter, create bold new opportunities for us, and equip us to move forward to the 21st century with confidence."), but you don't share the enthusiasm.

"What's great about this?" you ask yourself. "And why on earth does that guy sound so happy? He's describing an earthquake. I'm supposed to find that exciting?"

You wish it would all just go away.

But you realize that it won't.

You really have no choice.

You've just had a wake-up call.

*Change is in the air, and things will* **never be the same.**

**WHEN WE** hear this alarm, many of us draw a quick and not altogether reassuring conclusion: we had no voice in the change that's going to affect us — we're not in control of our lives.

There is no escaping the fact that, at different times in our lives, each and every one of us will encounter situations where change envelops us with such force and gravity that we realize we aren't in control of our lives.

## LOSING CONTROL

These instances certainly aren't limited to work. A divorce, a serious illness, the death of a loved one: each represents a powerful change we may feel powerless to affect or influence.

Nor is the sense of lost control limited to change that is imposed from the outside. Even when we initiate change ourselves (and assume that we'll be in charge because it was our choice), the results or implications of our decisions can extend well beyond our ability to control them.

A couple decides to have a child, for example, planning, saving for, and anticipating the event that many believe represents one of life's most rewarding experiences. The happy day arrives, the new family member comes home, and the world is turned upside down.

Mom and Dad feel permanently exhausted. Simple pleasures like going out to a movie on the spur of the moment are no longer options. There's no time for old friends (who, unless they're also new parents, may not be interested in talk about diapers and midnight feedings, anyway). The parents conclude, "We've lost control of our lives."

### It feels like
*we've been on the Space Mountain ride at Disneyland with the lights off and I can't get out of my seat...*

Employee during plant closing

**WHEN WE** perceive that we've lost control, the impact is likely to be significant and unsettling. We feel we've been attacked; the most common and immediate response is, "I'd better fight back."

But identifying a villain isn't always easy. In business, for example, while it's convenient

### FIGHTING BACK

to single out "the company" for blame, that may not always be accurate. When we think things are out of control, we'd like to think that the organizations we work for are omnipotent and all–seeing. In fact, like individuals, their actions can sometimes be determined by external forces over which they have little control. If RBS Inc. (Really Big Shoe) determines that it has to exit the galoshes business because people no longer wear galoshes, for instance, who is there to attack?

Finding someone or something to attack can be downright problematical. Who's responsible for floods and earthquakes? If your best friend is diagnosed with cancer, who takes the blame?

**Whose fault is it that the new parents can't go to the movies? The baby's?**

# *understanding*

## THE DYNAMICS

## OF CHANGE

## AND

## TRANSITION

RATHER THAN getting caught up in who did what to whom and why, we propose to focus on what we've come to realize is a far more productive alternative: understanding change and then figuring out how to function when it occurs. Rather than chaining ourselves to the causes of change, we can focus on the consequences of change. That's where the leverage is, and that's how we can use change to our advantage.

Once they've gotten a little sleep, for example, our new parents might review both the positive and negative consequences of their beautiful little (in size, not impact) change. On the plus side they might list, "A new person to love, hug, brag about, teach to ride a horse (or hit a curve ball)." On the minus side they might add, "No time alone with each other," "Miss our friends," or "Conversation restricted to baby topics."

Then they might work on the troublesome aspects of change. Perhaps they resolve to find a responsible baby–sitter for a couple of hours two evenings a week. Suppose they can't find or can't afford a good sitter. Maybe they could find another couple willing to share sitting duties so that they, too, can get off on their own for a few hours. Perhaps our couple makes two new friends in the process. Perhaps all four decide to expand the arrangement as their children get a bit older, creating a morning play group for a group of kids monitored by a rotating cast of parents. The negatives of change seem to be dropping away, and they may even be turning into additional positives.

## WHAT CHANGE IS

**TO USE** change to our advantage, we'll need to agree on several truths about change.

## Truth: *Change Is Natural*

One thing we know about change is that it's a natural force. Think of night and day. Think of birth, growth, and death. Think of the changing seasons. Think of the passage of time. Think of revolutions. Think of evolution.

## Truth: *Change Is Constant*

"Nothing endures but change," the philosopher Heraclitus observed, supporting his argument with the intriguing observation, "It is not possible to step twice into the same river." Whether we choose to acknowledge the fact or not, everyone and everything is always changing. Arguing against change is like arguing against breathing.

## Truth: Change Is Necessary

Without change, there can be no life, growth, renewal, invention, creativity, or evolution. The absence of change doesn't bring peace or comfort; it's more accurately a sign of stagnation or death.

Imagine a stock exchange in which there is no change. There's no market; it's an ex–stock exchange! Think about a company that never introduces a new product. Ask yourself how new companies could ever emerge if they didn't offer new ideas, changing things to improve on the past.

## Truth: Change Is a Catalyst

Change is a catalyst that can inspire opportunity or danger, good or evil, creation or destruction. In and of itself it is neutral, neither positive nor negative, but it nevertheless can unleash a range of powerful forces.

People often influence or shape those forces. Think of the mother who reacted to a horrible change — the death of her child by an intoxicated motorist — by creating a grassroots movement against drunk driving.

Sometimes, even a small action can have tremendous consequences. An individual who takes a career assessment may begin a journey into a whole new career path.

## Truth: *Change is Unpredictable*

Whenever things change, we can only be sure of one thing: they'll never be the same again. Change sets off a variety of responses in the different systems it touches, and, at the outset, we can never be certain what those responses will be.

When programmers set out to design a new software package, for example, they spend months or even years developing all the useful and necessary features they believe the program should contain. Once they've completed their efforts, they go back to work in search of things that, without their knowledge, have crept into the software during the development process.

Actions in one area (or several parts) of the software inevitably have unanticipated consequences in other parts. Often these take the form of "bugs," problems or glitches that need to be isolated and then removed from the software without harming the intended features. (At other times the process reveals that useful, but unplanned, items have actually found their way into the program. The designers "document" these features, announcing, in effect, "Yeah, well you know we meant to do that all along.")

**When
development
efforts
fall far
behind schedule,
it is often
because
insufficient
attention
has been
paid to the
unpredictable
nature of**
*change.*

# What Hasn't Changed

All these change truths
share at least one attribute:
**there's nothing new** ◄----------------------
----------------------► **about any of them.**
When we're confronted
with change today,
we're not facing a
revolutionary new phenomenon.
We've been dealing with change
throughout and
in all parts of our lives,
and it hasn't changed
its essential form or nature
since the beginning of time.

# WHAT HAS CHANGED

NOT EVEN change is immune to change — and what has changed the most is its pace. Not too long ago, for example, if someone asked, "Where's the report you promised me?" we could say, "It's in the mail," then complete the report, then really put it into the mail, and probably get away with it. That worked until affordable air courier service arrived on the scene...and fax machines... and e–mail, so that today it seems that we have no place to hide.

Or, think of television sets. They haven't changed too much over the years. At one time we received 10 or 12 channels through antennas. Then, hooked to cable systems, we got 30, 40, or even 50 channels of programs. Today, cable systems and satellite companies offer 100 or 150 channels, and there is talk of systems delivering 500 different channels in the near future. Where will we find time to watch it all? How will we even figure out what there is to watch?

This continually increasing level makes change seem particularly ominous or overwhelming. But we can deal with that, developing skills that allow us to take advantage of the powerful, renewing force of change. If we can figure out the 500–channel television system, we're sure to find new, unexpected, and valuable resources hidden within it.

**THE DAYS** of a single monumental change, followed by a relatively calm and lengthy adjustment period (allowing people to acclimate to the new situation), followed by a return to a long and reassuring period of "normalcy" are no longer with us.

Their place has been taken by an environment of continual change, where, often as not, one change initiative reveals the need for further change, and that, in turn, identifies opportunities for additional innovation, and so forth and so on, non-stop.

## I feel like
*an average skier who's been led to a Black Diamond Slope. I'm scared and excited... I'm thrilled, but the experience feels foreign — I hope I make it through the run...*

Employee during re-engineering

Thanks, perhaps, to companies that avoided change until they had no other option, change has often been interpreted historically as a response to a crisis or problem. No more. Leading companies have decided that change offers a way to stay ahead of competitors, helping organizations anticipate and take advantage of opportunities before they're forced to respond to problems.

In this context, change ceases to be a destination and becomes a constant journey. If — as individuals or as organizations — we're slow or unwilling or unable to react and adapt, we're likely to be overwhelmed by subsequent waves of change before we've been able to deal conclusively with the original event. We may never catch up.

That's not a good situation, not for the companies we work for, not for the people we work with, and certainly not for ourselves.

## CHANGE AND TRANSITION

TO KEEP pace with change and respond realistically and effectively, we actually need to think in terms of two phenomena: change and transition.

In this context, we think of change as an event or events: beginnings, endings, or significant alterations in the course of something. Transition reflects the period of adjustment during which people come to terms with the consequences of change events.

Change events can usually be associated with a specific time: the date on which you close the purchase of a house, for example, or the point at which the merger of two companies is formalized. Transition tends to be much less precise.

Once you take ownership of the new house, for example, when does it become your "home"? You might complete the transition as you complete the transaction, saving your money, finding just the right place, spending all your free hours choosing draperies, gleefully sending the landlord of the apartment you've occupied for all these years your final rent check, and popping the cork on a bottle of champagne on the day you move in.

Or you might need months to get used to the new place, re-papering the dining room four times before it's "right," never quite figuring out what switch controls which light, wondering if you'll ever get to know your new neighbors (and worrying that they'll never take the place of your "old" next–door neighbors), even returning home from work to discover that you've unconsciously driven to your old home.

You may never recognize exactly when the transition to life in your new house is complete. But at some point, you sense that the new place "just feels like home."

But wait a minute. It's not just you in this new house, it's you and your spouse. You both need to make the psychological and emotional adjustment to your new home for the transition to be complete, and your husband is having a harder time of it. He really misses the best friend he used to live next door to, he thinks there's too much traffic in the new neighborhood, he finds the property taxes astonishing, and he's beginning to think that it was a mistake to move.

But he senses that you like your new home, and he honestly doesn't want to ruin things for you, so he's keeping quiet, which means that you're not aware of his misgivings. So you don't understand why he keeps promising, and then keeps postponing, a trip to the nursery with you to look at shrubs for your new backyard. But you're beginning to lose patience.

And what about your daughter? Granted, she's 15, so

there's no way to know very much about what she's thinking and feeling, but she's been particularly quiet lately. In fact, she's just learned from her best friend (at her old school) that her boyfriend has spent his lunch period with the same girl for the last three days running. Your daughter knows this wouldn't have happened if she hadn't been forced to move.

## I feel like

*Christopher*
*Columbus,*
*out to sea*
*for awhile,*
*the crew is*
*threatening*
*mutiny*
*and I'm hoping*
*to see*
*land soon...*

Employee in culture change

Change and transition can be just as complex at work, even in what may seem to be simple situations. Suppose that a new telephone system with advanced voice-mail capabilities is installed in your office. People who are already busy will have to learn to use it, and then they'll have to become comfortable enough with the system to use it consistently and productively.

It's likely that a few individuals will embrace the new system immediately. Their fingers will flash across the keypad as they figure out how to retrieve messages, delete some, add comments to others, forward the results automatically to six different people, record a message and distribute it to an entire department, and so forth.

A few others will probably decide (but may not announce) that they don't care what anyone says, they're "not gonna use this new system, period." Perhaps they think there's already too much technology in their lives, and that if they let these robots invade one more corner of their existence, the scales will be tipped, and life will simply become too mechanical to enjoy. They may want to talk to "real, live" people, or they may worry that important messages won't ever be heard by anyone.

Most individuals will land somewhere between these two extremes. They'll be hesitant and uncertain about the new system at first but will gradually come to understand and accept it, until, at some as yet undefined point in the future, when the voice-mail system breaks down (and it will), they'll wonder how they ever got the job done without it.

Given the range of probable responses, the change can only be considered complete when enough people make enough of a commitment to use the phone system so that the original objective for installing it is met. This doesn't mean that everyone has to buy in, just enough users to make the system genuinely useful. (When that does occur, the people who originally resolved to ignore the change will probably have to re-evaluate their decision if they wish to remain productive, or if they wish to remain at all.)

We can begin to see just how intricate transitions can become for organizations, from families to multinational corporations, and for the individuals that comprise them.

How do we deal with this complexity? One way to understand transitions is by breaking the process down into parts.

# THE THREE PHASES OF TRANSITION

IT TURNS out that, no matter how many transitions we examine, we can identify a recurring three-stage pattern that characterizes them all. Whether the transition is introduced by change that we welcome, are ambivalent about, or are actively opposed to, we need to pass through three distinct phases to complete the process successfully. We call these stages Endings, Exploration, and New Beginnings.

During the Endings phase, we confront the conclusion of familiar things, a task that often means dealing with strong emotions. Before we can consider the future in times of change, we have to let go of the past, accepting the loss of old and comfortable ways.

Next comes Exploration, when we begin to reorient ourselves to the new situation, considering options and opportunities. This is typically a time of uncertainty, turmoil, and even chaos as we find ourselves being pulled between the past and the future, embracing change tentatively and then recoiling back toward a more familiar and, we perceive, a more comfortable past. Somewhat paradoxically, it's also a period of real opportunity: detached from familiar ways, remarkably creative responses often emerge from our situation.

If we make our way successfully through the first two stages of transition, we enter the third phase, New Beginnings. By reaching this point, we show that we're ready to move forward to re-engage the new situation. We feel reasonably comfortable about the future and our place in it, and we can begin to reassume a role as an active contributor.

Change events inevitably introduce transition experiences, whether we want, anticipate, plan for, or even try to deny them.

# THE TRANSITIONAL TRAPEZE

TO GET a clearer image of the transition process, sit back for a minute and imagine you're dreaming. You find yourself standing alone on a small platform, high above the sawdust floor of a packed and noisy circus tent. A spotlight swings up to illuminate you against the darkness at the top of the tent, and the crowd quiets.

A trapeze bar swings to and fro in front of you. Off in the distance, someone you can't quite make out stands on another platform, holding a second trapeze and watching you intently. You've never been on a trapeze, but the crowd seems to expect that that's just what you'll do. Climbing down the rope ladder to the sawdust arena floor doesn't seem like an acceptable option.

The ringmaster looks skyward and announces, "And now ladies and gentlemen, boys and girls, please direct your attention to 'The Daring Young Performer on the Transitional Trapeze...'"

You flex your knees, rub your hands together, and realize that if you actually grasp the trapeze and leave the comparative safety of the platform to swing out into space, the next thing you're going to have to do is let go of the bar to jump to the second trapeze. The idea inspires two questions… life-and-death questions.

First, will the second bar be where you need it when you need it? You realize the answer to this question rests in that mysterious other person's hands, someone you don't even know! You'll have lost control of the situation, you'll be at the mercy of someone else. Can you really be sure that he or she has your best interests at heart?

Second, is there a net beneath you? You look down. Yes, there's something there, and it sure looks like a net, but is it in the right place, and will it support your weight, and how competent or attentive were the people who put it up?

The crowd begins to clap rhythmically, and a voice floats up: "Go on, do it!" You take a deep breath, think, "I must be out of my mind," and then grab the first trapeze, letting go and taking off in search of the second.

You've just completed

**the Endings phase**

of your transition.

At the very instant you leave the platform, your entire being focuses on a single, overwhelming goal: connecting. You feel as if you're looking in all directions at the same time, riveted to the smallest detail and considering the faintest possibility in your search for renewed stability. (If this were a movie, the scene would unfold in slow motion.) You think for a moment about returning to where you came from, but just as quickly realize that the trapeze won't swing back that far.

This is precisely what people feel during
**Exploration.**

Finally you let go of the first bar, catch the second trapeze, and swing safely to the far platform. The audience roars. You're shaking like a leaf, but you also feel a tremendous sense of relief, accomplishment, and excitement. You also sense that, while you might not want to repeat the experience any time soon, you could do it again.

**You're in New Beginnings.**

However melodramatic our example may seem, real-life transitions often turn out to be far more compelling and emotional for the individuals who complete them. Think back to adolescence, and you can probably identify a number of transitions that, when you originally faced them, seemed a lot more dangerous than a trapeze ride. Or, what if a dramatic reorganization changes your job and work environment so profoundly that you're not quite sure if you're still working for the same company? The sense of dislocation and uncertainty about the future can be debilitating. Life — not just your business life — can seem thoroughly out of control.

*personal*

RESPONSES

TO

CHANGE

ONE DANGER of making any generalization about change — and that's what the above observation is, a generalization introduced to illustrate a broad point — is that it may suggest there is one "best" way to react to change. That's not true. We all respond to change in complex ways that are ultimately unique to ourselves. It's part of what makes us individuals.

We've already suggested, for example, that different people have different reactions to the same change event and, as a result, different transition experiences. A number of factors combined to create these personal change profiles.

## NATURAL RESPONSES: INNOVATORS, ADAPTERS, AND TRADITIONALISTS

Some of us embrace change whole-heartedly and virtually automatically. We come home from a hard day at work and relax by rearranging the living room. The fact that the personal computer we own meets all our needs doesn't stop us from shopping for a newer, more powerful machine. We might be called Innovators.

Some of us prefer life to be stable and predictable. Maintaining traditions may be very important for us. We find real value in "holding down the fort." We might call ourselves Traditionalists.

Most of us sit somewhere on a spectrum that spans these two extremes. We understand the value of tradition, but we're ultimately willing and able to adapt to change when we encounter it. It's not too big a deal for some of us (we're relatively closer to the furniture movers on the change continuum), or maybe it isn't all that easy ( we're closer to the Traditionalists' end). But, one way or another, we can and do adapt. So we'll call ourselves Adapters.

Generally speaking (uh-oh, another generalization) and all other things being equal (which, in complex situations, they rarely are), Innovators complete transitions more quickly than Traditionalists, and Adapters complete them at rates somewhere between those of the other two groups.

This doesn't mean that Innovators are "good" or that Traditionalists are "bad," however. Innovators can be loose cannons or worthy champions of change. Traditionalists can derail necessary change initiatives or protect organizations from ill-conceived efforts. When an investment bank or brokerage firm with a centuries-old reputation discovers that a rogue trader (an Innovator, perhaps?) has quietly run up a couple of hundred million dollars in losses without telling anyone, the organization's leaders may wish that they'd listened — or given a greater voice — to people in their ranks (Traditionalists, maybe?) who would have said, "That's not how we do things here."

## PERCEPTIONS OF SPECIFIC CHANGE EVENTS

The manner in which we perceive our ability to handle a specific change event also has an important impact on our response to change. We might be extremely confident about mastering the numerous complexities of a new job, for example, but be terrified of making a five–minute oral presentation on a topic that's already familiar to us. Our ability to complete transitions smoothly is enhanced in situations where we feel we possess the ability to manage or master the change.

There's another important aspect to this. When something changes, we don't necessarily react to what happened or to what others may have intended to happen. We react to what we think was done or intended. In times of change, perception equals reality.

Here's a business example. A company with offices in a number of different cities announced a restructuring designed to let the organization serve clients more efficiently. Employees appeared to accept and adapt to the change smoothly, except in one office, where business ground to a halt. It turned out that the people in that office believed that the restructuring announcement was going to be followed by a major downsizing. They even "knew" that the official word would come down on a Thursday (although they didn't know which Thursday), and so they were spending their time preparing for what they now called "Black Thursday."

The company had no such plans. In fact management saw a need to hire additional employees. But until the people in that one office could be convinced that no cuts were planned, they had a very different perception of — and reaction to — change than did their colleagues elsewhere in the organization.

## I feel like
*I'm at a magic show — what you see is not what you get.*

Employee in restructure

## EVALUATION OF LOSSES AND GAINS

When we encounter change situations, most of us take a quick personal survey. What are we likely to gain as a result of this change? What might we lose? When we assess our answers, do we perceive a threat or an opportunity? Our conclusions are likely to affect our transition response.

Here's an example: a company introduces a change to "empower employees."

One employee — let's call him Joe — looks at the situation and sees trouble. He worries that he may have to give up power or responsibility to others in the new environment. From Joe's perspective, the phrase "employee empowerment" has a sinister ring to it. He isn't about to go off and sabotage the effort, but we probably shouldn't expect him to champion it either.

Another employee, Jane, interprets the phrase "empowerment" enthusiastically. She anticipates new opportunities opening up within the organization and believes that she has the skills and experience to take advantage of them. We might expect Jane to embrace change readily and complete the transition process relatively quickly.

Our reaction to specific change events is also influenced by our cumulative experience of change. If we've encountered a great deal of change in our lives, successfully navigating some pretty rough waters in the process, we may become "change-resilient." We trust our ability to respond to change, interpreting it to be a valuable skill that we've developed. This helps us believe that we'll deal successfully with change now and in the future, no matter what comes our way.

You may have heard someone remember childhood as an "Army brat," a life spent in constant motion, leaving one part of the country or world for another at a moment's notice, having to adapt to new schools and make new friends time and again. Often such people sum up the experience by observing, "After that, and to this day, new situations just never bothered me that much."

Our personal change history may not have inspired resilience, however. If we look back through our catalog of life events and decide that most or all of them have been failures, we may conclude that we, too, are failures or victims. The possibility of another change "shockwave" can send us running for cover. Transition is likely to be a difficult — perhaps even an impossible — process if we cling to this perspective. Another Army brat might tell you, "If I'd just had some roots, stayed in one place for longer than a year, I'd be much more comfortable with change today."

## CURRENT CHANGE LEVELS

Nothing says that change will wait for a time that's convenient for us. Change events are just as likely to appear concurrently as consecutively.

Completing the transition to a new job is one thing. Completing that transition when your daughter is about to leave home for college, your brother's marriage is coming apart, and you're anxiously awaiting bank approval for the home-equity loan that will let you pay your child's tuition... well that's something else entirely.

There can be such a thing as change overload, where the combined "weight" of change makes dealing with any one part of it a significant challenge.

# A PERSONAL CHANGE PROFILE

**IF WE** examine our lives through a prism shaped by the kinds of forces, influences, and life experiences introduced above, we can begin to develop a personal change profile. This is an inventory of self-knowledge that shows where we stand in relation to change at any given time and explains why we occupy that position.

It can be a calming and reassuring process. When we're uncomfortable with, or feel threatened by, change — but don't really understand why — it's easy to assume the worst: we can't keep up, this is going to be a disaster. But when we take stock, we often discover that the discomfort we feel is, in fact, entirely reasonable and thoroughly understandable. We may learn that we've never been completely comfortable with change. We may realize that, in addition to this change event, we're also beginning an exciting, but unfamiliar, new personal relationship, and we're feeling stretched by the business course we've signed up for. If we weren't uncomfortable, there'd be something wrong with us.

Understanding where we stand with change serves another important purpose. It creates a baseline, a point of departure that begins to show whether, and how, we might think of changing our change profile.

**IT'S A** fact. Because we're always changing (you'll recall that nothing escapes change), because we're able to receive new information, and because we're capable of making choices, we can get "better" at changing. We can alter our change profile to raise our comfort level in times of change, improve our responses to change, and enhance our resilience to change events.

## CHANGING YOUR CHANGE PROFILE

To put this in perspective, think back to our discussion of change and transition for a moment. We called change a neutral, catalytic force that is beyond our control. We also said that, although neutral in and of itself, its catalytic powers can unleash powerful forces that are either positive or negative. And we said that change triggers transition, the process that represents our response to change.

This response — in other words, the shape or character of our transition — is determined by our perception of change. (Remember that, in time of change, perception equals reality.) It's the sum total of our values, beliefs, and attitudes toward change that determines our personal change profile… our perception of change.

For change to succeed, the transition process has to be completed. The three stages of Endings, Exploration, and New Beginnings can't be skipped or short-circuited. But transition can be made more manageable if we understand how it works and realize how we're likely to respond.

Transition, then, is not outside our influence. We can't do much about change, but we can do a lot with transition. Since it's our personal change profile that determines our response to the dual nature of change — whether we interpret it as a good or bad thing, an ally or an enemy — if we change our profile, we change our entire experience of change.

We've already mentioned a number of different transition responses anecdotally. Now let's take a somewhat more organized approach, working our way through the stages of transition to identify typical responses. For simplicity and the sake of continuity, we'll talk a lot about change in a work setting, but any points we raise can be applied just as easily to transitions in other aspects of life.

# "What's Wrong with Me?"

WHAT ARE our own responses likely to be? For a start, let's consider one of the most common, the "What's Wrong with Me?" reaction.

Particularly in a task-oriented work environment, success or superior performance is frequently measured by the ability to take on assignments and complete them quickly and competently. If we apply this yardstick to transitions, we may conclude that anything less than complete and immediate acceptance of the new situation represents a personal and professional failure.

Perhaps we've reacted to change on a purely rational or intellectual level. "I see the need for that," we say. Or we decide, "I don't like it, but it's clear that I'll have to go along."

In any event, we almost certainly haven't completed (or perhaps even begun) our transition. We need to make an emotional move to the new situation, leaving the old behind and reconciling ourselves to new realities. We know that this requires an investment of time, attention, and effort.

So if we assume that we should complete a transition automatically and immediately, we're likely to frustrate ourselves, and we may even erect roadblocks that actually complicate and delay the transition.

# *personal*

## TRANSITION

## RESPONSES

**WHAT CAN** we do in this situation? First we can take a look at common responses to transition in sharper detail, thinking about them for each of the three stages of the transition process. This can give us a reasonable idea of where we are in transition. Then we can discuss the needs reflected by these responses. This offers a sense of direction, an idea of where we should be headed. Finally, we can introduce different kinds of actions that will help us meet our needs and address our responses to change.

## *Endings:* COMMON RESPONSES

"I'm listening to a tornado alert and telling myself, 'This can't be happening here.'"

"I'm blindfolded."

"It's not my party and I'm not going."

We've said that the Endings phase of a transition involves letting go of familiar things or situations. For most of us, this produces strong emotions.

Denial is a typical response to the uncertainty that initially accompanies change. We may focus on the things that have stayed the same in our lives in the wake of change. This lets us deny the need to change and, in some cases, enables us to refuse to admit that change has even occurred.

Another common response is resistance. Like the employee who resolves not to use the new voice-mail system, we simply refuse to go along with change. Resistant behavior can be confrontational and argumentative, or it can be passive, like when someone acts as if he or she agrees with a new policy but does little or nothing to implement it. Resistance differs from denial in that resistant people know that change is taking place but decide that the new rules don't apply to them.

Other common reactions include anxiety, anger, and confusion. When friends and colleagues lose their jobs as part of change, we may also express sadness and "survivor's guilt," for example. To move onward, we obviously need to reconcile ourselves to these feelings of loss.

# *Endings:* NEEDS

If we examine this range of typical responses to the Endings phase of transition, we find that they reflect two broad needs: the need for empathy, and the need for validation.

**Empathy.** We need people to understand how we feel during the Endings phase. We want our response to the situation to be acknowledged by others. If we're angry, it helps to hear someone say, "You must be really mad." If we hurt, we want our pain to be acknowledged. If we're fearful, it helps to be told, "It sounds really scary."

It's not a matter of getting people to agree with us. Our immediate need is for them to hear what we're saying and sense what we're feeling.

**Validation.** During the Endings period, we often interpret change as a personal indictment, a rejection of past practices. "They're telling us we've been doing things wrong all along," we may think. "If we weren't, why would they want us to change?"

What we need in this environment is validation, the understanding that what we've done in the past was good, not bad. It was right for its time, but times have changed, and now new approaches are required. We need to be able to honor the past, telling ourselves — and believing it — "What I was and what I did was okay."

## Endings: ENHANCING THE TRANSITION

There are things we can do to help meet these needs and ease the process of letting go. Like our hypothetical new parents, we can identify and articulate the kinds of problems or losses that change has introduced to our lives. If we sense that gains are also involved, we should remind ourselves of them as well.

To do this effectively, we need to find ways to express our feelings about the situation openly and honestly. If we're dealing with change at work, we may find that the company has set up workshops or created other outlets to help deal with the situation. Some employers even schedule "gripe" sessions, where individuals can air anger, fear, and other emotions in a safe environment. Or, a spouse or close friend might make a good audience, listening to our concerns or complaints.

Many people find that creating or observing some form of ceremony eases the process of letting go. We're all familiar with formal rituals (from weddings to wakes to commencement exercises) that people use, not just to introduce something new, but to commemorate and let go of the past as well. Less formally, what do we do when a love affair ends? Why we take all the old love letters and burn them! The process helps us air anger or sadness and let go of the past.

Similar events can help us deal with the Ending stage at work. After a major change has been announced, our department might schedule a "Trash Day," for example, during which everyone spends his or her time throwing away old files that are no longer needed as a way of letting go. Or, suppose the facility we work at is scheduled to close down, scattering people we've been associated with for years, some to new jobs, some to new careers. We might plan a farewell dinner to mark this passing and encourage people to share memories as a way of "letting go" while recognizing great success.

Talking through the events that surround change helps us internalize and come to grips with the situation. This can be particularly valuable in work settings, since it helps us move away from the, "After all we've done for them, look at what they did to us," kind of thinking that focuses on the cause of change (which we can't control), rather than on its consequences (which we can influence).

But we also need to set aside time for personal reflection. What does all this mean? How does it affect our feelings about ourself and our employer? What might we be able to "hold onto"? Our personal values, our professionalism, our pride, for example.

When those feelings include sadness or anger, it's important to let our emotions surface. The purpose of letting go isn't to be polite or tough, it's to sort through and familiarize ourselves with the range of conflicting feelings and emotions that we're likely to exhibit in such a tumultuous setting. The more we're able to open ourselves up to the situation, the sooner we begin to come to terms with it. We may feel a little more comfortable or optimistic about the future and our place in it. We'll still have concerns, but we'll begin to start looking around to see not only what has been left behind but also what has taken its place.

At some point, most of us find that we are beginning to feel resigned to the new situation. We've thought, we've

## Endings:
### PERSONAL STRATEGIES

- Give the ending a name.
- Communicate your feelings with the people in your life.
- Give the situation time.
- Talk to people you trust for support.
- Focus on the future, not the past.
- Keep in touch with your thoughts.
- Separate yourself from the job you've been doing.
- Acknowledge the value of the past.
- Look for the positive things that are happening.

worried, we've talked about change, and it's become more familiar. We've realized that this is the way our world is going to be, at least until the next change. That's a signal that the Endings phase is drawing to a conclusion for us.

**I feel**
*stressed*
*and tired,*
*like I'm going*
*up the down*
*escalator...*

Employee during realignment

# *Exploration:* COMMON RESPONSES

"I feel like a pinball bouncing off the walls of the machine, trying to stay in the game, hoping not to drop into the hold."

"I'm at a crossroads."

"I've jumped from the plane, but I don't know if the parachute will work."

In the Exploration stage of transition, as we begin to reorient ourselves to our new situation, we tend to make conflicting responses.

We test the new realities we've identified, comparing them to the more familiar conditions they are replacing. We may find ourselves approaching the new situation tentatively and then recoiling back toward the more familiar and comfortable circumstances we've been asked to put behind us.

We're ambivalent. We're struggling to believe in and adapt to the new, but there are still times when we wish for "the good old days." So we feel optimistic and energized at one moment and angry or frustrated the next.

Our performance and concentration levels suffer as we swing from one pole to the other.

Chaos and confusion are common responses to Exploration. Should we focus on the dangers or the opportunities associated with change? Will we think in terms of perceived losses or potential gains?

Creativity is another important reaction as we begin to apply undirected energy to consider possibilities in the new or emerging environment.

This is a crucial point in the transition process. How we respond can have major implications in terms of how smoothly we'll complete the full transition.

## *Exploration:* Needs

The ambivalence and uncertainty typically associated with Exploration identifies three basic needs: information, communication, and structure.

**Information.** Knowledge is power during Exploration. The more accurate our information about the change, the greater our ability to resolve uncertainty and move forward with our lives.

In the absence of good information about the need for, the process of, and our progress toward change, we tend to think the worst about a situation (often broadcasting our concerns as rumors). If we know the truth, and even if we don't like it, things almost always appear better than they do in its absence.

**Communication.** We also need good communication, which, since it's a two-way process of talking and listening, isn't the same as information. It's information transmitted, received, and responded to. If someone hands us a memo describing change, that isn't communication. There needs to be some kind of feedback loop to "hear" our reaction and incorporate our response in the change process.

**Structure.** Finally, the Exploration phase signals the time when we need a framework or structure introduced (or reintroduced) to our lives. As we struggle to choose between the past and the future, a clear sense of what awaits us helps us gain and maintain momentum.

# I feel like

*I'm in a hot air balloon — I was afraid on the way up; now I'm having fun because I'm flying high!*

Employee in new job

# *Exploration:* ENHANCING THE TRANSITION

An important goal during Exploration is to develop and maintain a commitment to moving forward. Focusing on the gains and opportunities change offers helps many people commit. It's usually a lot easier to keep going, after all, when we anticipate rewards.

In the work environment, companies can help by pre-senting — and repeating again and again — a vision of the organization's future. You might even attempt to identify that vision on your own. What will the priorities be? Are there new objectives? Have key skills been rede-fined? Where is future growth and profit-ability likely to come from? The more you learn (or even assume) about the company's future, the more likely you are to identify interesting opportunities for yourself.

It may also help to remind ourselves that, once change occurs, things can never be the same again. There's no going back on the transitional trapeze, so our only realistic option is to keep moving forward.

Another important tactic during Exploration involves finding ways to assert some degree of control over the situation. We've talked about the loss of control that change introduces by launching us into unfamiliar new territory. This can paralyze us: we're not sure what to do, and so we do as little as possible until we're able to better understand what's taking place.

To begin to move ahead again with our lives and careers, we need to re-establish a sense of control, the feeling that we can have an effect on what is happening around us. This is unlikely to be an all-or-nothing event, however. We begin somewhat tentatively and then, as we become more familiar and comfortable in our new surroundings, take more aggressive initiatives.

A good tactic for beginning to reestablish control of the situation is to identify and focus on things that we can control and, to the extent that it's possible, ignore everything else. If we can't do anything about something, we don't fret about it. We concentrate on areas, however few there may be initially, over which we have some degree of control.

In addition, we may find that setting priorities for ourselves, identifying options that are available, and determining new ways to make ourselves valuable in the changed environment will also help us establish a degree of control.

Activities like these help to create the sense of structure that is so useful during Exploration. Another source of structure is internal: our own values. Even when everything else in life seems to be changing rapidly, our

- Build temporary structures.
- Broaden your focus.
- Talk to people for ideas, support, and information.
- Test your skills in new areas.
- Share expertise with others.
- Learn new things.
- Read.
- Don't act for the sake of action.
- Celebrate small achievements.
- Spend time alone to relax and think.
- Take care of yourself.
- Set short–term goals and timetables.
- Do small things well.
- Look around to see what's out there.
- Find out what's new in the new environment.

personal values tend to remain constant. Examining and referring to them can offer a reassuring anchor during the tumultuous times of this phase.

As we continue the process of Exploration and begin to feel more at home in our new setting, it becomes important to challenge ourselves. Change tests many things: our skills, experience, flexibility, and determination. To complete the transition, we need to face these challenges.

Establishing a set of personal development objectives offers an appropriate method for challenging yourself. Based on the understanding of new conditions that you've developed, what personal factors for future success are likely to be important? What objectives can you set for yourself to take advantage of this knowledge?

# *New Beginnings:* COMMON RESPONSES

> "I've crossed over a very deep gorge on a very rickety bridge."

> "I feel like a volcano has erupted and lava has beenflowing; now it has stopped and new life has the opportunity to grow on fertile ground."

Finally we reach the ultimate stage of transition, New Beginnings. We begin to recommit ourselves to life in its new and changed form.

As we reorient ourselves, we start to put feelings of conflict behind us. Our activities are marked by actions directed toward achieving success in the new setting. As we set new priorities, identify new goals, and develop new alliances, our perspective shifts from the past to the future. We feel more enthusiastic and energetic than we have in some time.

# *New Beginnings:* NEEDS

The two needs most often associated with New
Beginnings, Participation and Alignment, are actually
vital in all three phases of transition but become particularly important if we're to finish the process successfully.

**Participation.** This is the time when we need to stop
analyzing things or preparing ourselves and start trans-
lating ideas into action. If we're dealing with change in an
organization, we need to be given the opportunity to par-
ticipate. But here, as in any change setting, we also need
to make a personal commitment to get involved and stay
active.

**Alignment.** Our personal response to change affects
— and is affected by — people or groups of people
around us. As we start to connect with the future in the
New Beginnings phase, we need to gain a sense that our
response to the situation is consistent or compatible
with — but not necessarily the same as — the goals and
objectives of the organization.

## New Beginnings:
### ENHANCING THE TRANSITION

This is the time to begin thinking about practical steps that can help us complete the transition successfully. We might list key steps we believe we'll need to complete to continue to move forward, for example. We can identify various forms of support we think we'll require to finish the transition process.

Thinking in terms of specific actions (not broad needs) and setting firm timetables (not hazy estimates) helps us put a period of dramatic change behind us and focus on the new opportunities that lie ahead.

**I feel like**
*I've always been a bird in a cage — now the door is open and I wonder, what's outside?*

Employee in a restructure

We'll need to begin to connect or re-connect with the new environment. At work, this is primarily a process of building new networks and creating new alliances as we begin to understand where we fit into the new system.

In most careers, developing networks and alliances typically becomes an organic process. As we're assigned new tasks, we identify resources that may be able to help us complete them. At the same time, we, ourselves, are also identified as useful resources by others. As our experience grows over the years, our system of alliances expands. We rely on existing networks to expand our contacts or develop new ones.

But in periods of abrupt change, old networks frequently fail to serve new realities. We need to recreate new alliances — and we need to do it as rapidly as possible — if we're to get back to working productively in the redesigned system.

## New Beginnings:
### PERSONAL STRATEGIES

- Experiment with new patterns before settling into a routine.
- Celebrate your progress.
- Slow down… enjoy the "newness."
- Notice differences.
- Visualize success in the new situation.
- Set new priorities.
- Keep your eyes open to opportunity.
- Translate ideas into actions.
- Communicate by listening as well as talking.
- Seek feedback.
- Keep in touch with old friends.
- Be optimistic.
- Stop preparing… Act!

The company may help. Employee teams may be created and assigned specific tasks. Networking opportunities may be presented through meetings and seminars.

But keep in mind that the responsibility for developing a new support structure within your organization ultimately falls to you. Don't be afraid to reach out to others. Realize that they are likely to be just as interested in creating new and useful alliances as you are.

## ALIGNMENT AND THE PACE OF TRANSITION

WHEN COMPANIES plan for major change, they sometimes assume — or hope — that the process will resemble a military parade: well-ordered groups of marchers (employees organized by business unit, subsidiary, or department, perhaps) will walk in step with one another, departing from the old situation to arrive at the new in the same orderly formation at a predetermined time.

But remember what we've learned about how different people react to change. In real life, group transitions aren't parades. They're more likely to resemble marathons involving thousands of competitors sprinting, or jogging, or plodding along at vastly different paces.

Innovators race ahead of the pack. Traditionalists remain at the starting line long after the starting gun has been fired. Adapters head off in the general direction of the finish, but some move more quickly than others. A few look back over their shoulders, wondering if the trip is a good idea. Some make detours, while others stop at the side of the road to rest or think about things. A couple may turn around, head back toward the starting line, and then, realizing that they are going against the flow of traffic, turn back again in the direction of change.

The innovators cross the finish line first, and some don't even seem to be breathing hard. The adapters arrive next, tired but exhilarated. Finally, as darkness falls, a pack of traditionalists crosses the finish line. They are exhausted, but they are also understandably proud of their achievement.

Now, and throughout transition, it can help if we remind ourselves that different people (including us) complete transitions at different speeds. If it seems that others are reconciling themselves to the new situation more quickly than we are, we shouldn't be overly concerned. This probably means only that it takes us somewhat longer to adapt to change. If we feel that others are taking to long to "get on board," on the other hand, we can pause to appreciate the challenges they may be facing.

## It seems like
*I'm just beginning to emerge from a cocoon — I feel good regarding my new roles and responsibilities.*

Manager in a merger

# CYCLING AND RECYCLING

FOR REASONS of brevity and clarity, these thoughts on change and transition are organized in linear fashion. This doesn't mean that transitions are linear processes. Remember the marathon metaphor: as some innovators are settling into new routines, late adapters may still be reconciling themselves with the past.

Or, if you think that you've made it past the Endings phase and have begun to concentrate on Exploration, but suddenly find that you've started to refocus on the past, don't be discouraged. Realize that transition is not a neat process: often a step forward is followed by two steps back. Eventually, however, if we stick with it, we complete transitions successfully.

Continual self-assessment helps us move the process along: Where are we today in the process? What situations or feelings can we anticipate at this point? In this way, we won't waste energy on, say, New Beginnings activities if we realize that we've have yet to complete the Exploration phase.

# CHANGE

# RESILIENCE:

# *thriving*

## AT THE

## EDGE OF

## CHANGE

THE TUMULTUOUS change so many of us experience at work today actually turns out to be good news if we can shift our thinking about our relationship to work and our employer. In the business world as it used to be, we essentially "sold" ourselves to a company in return for advancement, security, and retirement benefits.

A "good" employee was someone who would take any job, move anywhere, work for any boss, learn any skill, and so forth, and so on. In exchange for this "loyalty," he or she was virtually guaranteed a continuing relationship with the company.

In our new world of continual change and evolution, this kind of employer/employee relationship is simply no longer feasible. People who started their careers in the old system may say, "Hey! The rules changed in the middle of the game!" They're right, and, as a consequence, they may feel cheated.

Their reaction is totally understandable, but it misses the very real and very exciting possibilities that the new reality offers us.

In a world where relationships are shifting so dramatically, we have an opportunity to examine what work means to us as individuals. What are our special gifts, values, and beliefs? How do we want to express them in our lives, which, after all, are defined to one degree or another by the work we do? How can we use change resilience, a new sense of control in our careers, to let us explore new possibilities and take advantage of opportunities for greater self-expression in our careers?

In a world where employers can no longer depend on performance based on promises of security, there's a real need for new methods for achieving quality performance and productivity from the work force. In this new environment, the most valuable contributors will be looking, not for an environment of stability, but one that nourishes creativity and continuous growth.

In this new setting, "change-resilient" people are "career-resilient" people. In times of change, our "me" issues always surface first. Until they're resolved, we can't move forward to consider a broader career perspective.

But clearly it is becoming more and more important — essential, perhaps — for each of us to determine how to incorporate constant change into continued employability, career success, and personal satisfaction.

# I feel like

*I'm driving a car
without directions.
I'm either going
to get really lost
or have a
great adventure...*

Employee in a restructure

# WHAT'S
## *next*
## FOR
## YOU

**THE FOLLOWING** questions can be used to guide you as you go through current and future changes. You might want to write down your answers and use them to help you gain clarity and develop relevant and proactive strategies.

What is the change you are now experiencing?

Are you experiencing many changes at once?
What are they? How do they effect one another?

What is it that you are losing as a result of this change?

What might you gain as a result of this change?

What is ending for you?

What is not ending for you?

Who are the people that can support you through this change? What is it that you want them to do?

What is the best possible outcome of this change?
What can you do to bring it about?

What are the potential pitfalls?
How can you avoid or minimize them?

Where are you in your transition;
Endings, Exploration or New Beginnings?

## ENDINGS

What name can you give to this ending?

What are your feelings?  Who can you tell about them?

What can you do to take care of yourself?

What can you do to mentally mark this ending?

What are the positive things that are happening now?

## EXPLORATION

What temporary structure and routine can you set in place during this transition time?

What are the short-term goals you can achieve?

How will you celebrate and reward yourself for achieving your goals?

What new activities can you try?

What new skills can you learn?

## NEW BEGINNINGS

What is your version of success in this new situation?

What are your priorities?

What are the opportunities?

What actions do you need to take?

What feedback do you need?

# CONCLUSION

THE IDEAS and approaches introduced in this booklet are neither revolutionary nor particularly complicated. But they do produce results, and it is surprising how frequently they are overlooked in the confusing circumstances of major change.

We are beginning to realize that the only thing we know for sure about change is that, once it occurs, life will never be quite the same again. But we are also beginning to understand more and more about the dynamics of change and transition. We're realizing that people adapt to change differently, complete transitions at different speeds, and are affected by, and react to, change in different ways.

More to the point, we have identified methods we can employ as responsible individuals to help ourselves embrace change rather than fight it, complete transitions rather than be stalled by them, and, finally, commit ourselves to exploiting the opportunities presented by change rather than dwell on an irretrievable past.